Math, Reading, Art, Science & Spelling Games

ALL ABOUT OCEAN CREATURES

Master 80 Interesting Spelling Words
Practice Simple Addition and Multiplication

Learn About:

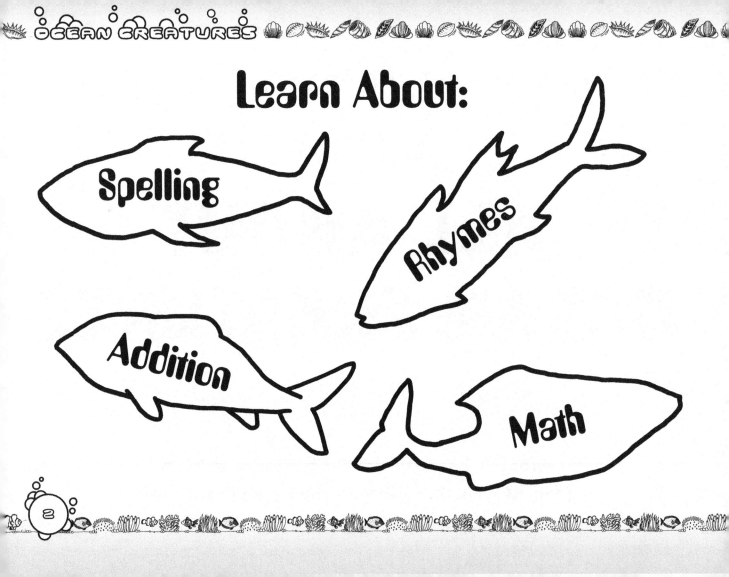

Spelling

Rhymes

Addition

Math

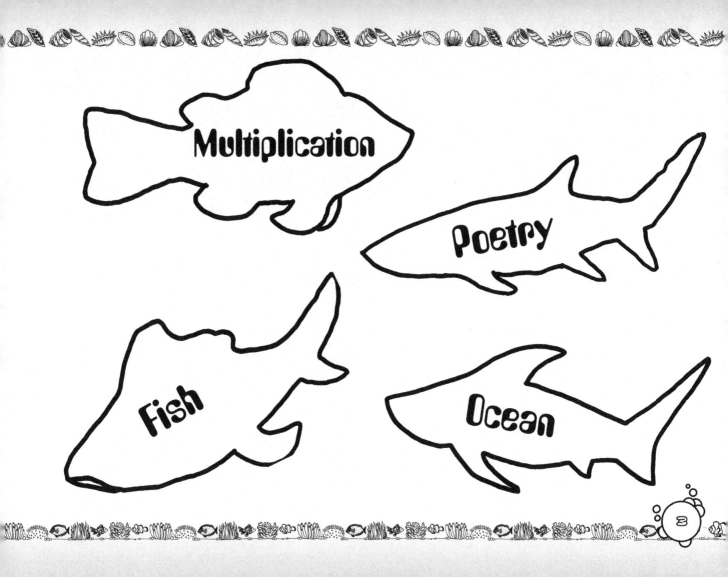

So Many Fish

Big fish, small fish
Thin fish, fat fish
Bluegill, red fish
Carp and catfish

Sharks and minnows
Dolphins, whales
Spiney fish
With crooked tails

Fill in the spaces with the words on the next page.

Big _____, small fish

Thin fish, fat fish

Bluegill, _____ fish

Carp and _____

Sharks and _____

Dolphins, whales

Spiney fish

With _____ tails

fish, car, red, green, catfish, dogfish, minnows, crayfish, crooked, long

Dan and Jill went to the City Aquarium. Dan saw three minnows, and Jill saw four dolphins.
How many animals did they see together?

Draw your answer.

SO MANY FISH

Match the rhyming pairs:

Sound	Wish
White	Tail
Clean	Reef
Teeth	Delight
Eight	Dream
Grab	Around
Fish	Loops
Hoops	Great
Whale	Place
Face	Crab

Dive deeper with these activities!

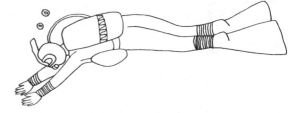

If you live near an ocean, ask an adult to take you fishing! Look up the different fish that you catch on Wikipedia.

Go to your local library and check out a book about the Pacific Ocean, the world's largest ocean. After reading it, tell someone about your favorite fact that you find in the book!

OCEAN CREATURES

The Shark

I am a shark

I have lots of teeth

I like to swim

Down near the reef

There are many kinds of sharks

Blue, tiger, and great white

We like to swim in oceans dark

It is our delight

Fill in the spaces with the words on the next page.

I'm a _____

I've lots of _____

I like to _____

Down near the _____

There are many kinds of sharks

Blue, _____, and great white

We like to swim in _____ dark

It is our _____

10

shark, frog, teeth, fins, swim, beef, reef, tiger, lion, baby, oceans, delight

OCEAN CREATURES

Carlos and Mary travel to the ocean and go looking for shark teeth on the beach. Carlos found ten, and Mary found thirteen.

How many teeth did they find together?

Draw your answer.

12

THE SHARK

Count the shark teeth.

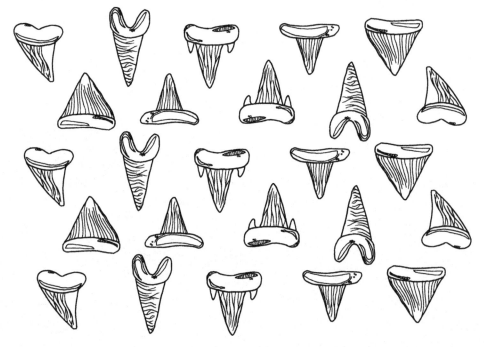

How many shark teeth are there? Write your answer here: _____

If you live near an ocean or take a vacation there, ask an adult to take you out to look for shark teeth.

Go to the library and find a book about sharks.

15

The Shrimp

Bonjour, my friend! I am a shrimp!
Though others like to call me "wimp",
I help a lot of other fish,
When clean scales is their wish.

Without me, the ocean's dirty.
That's why I like to clean.
Even today, on my birthday,
A clean ocean is my dream!

Fill in the spaces with the words on the next page.

_____, my friend! I am a _____!

Though others like to call me "wimp",

I help a lot of other _____,

When _____ scales is their wish.

Without me, the _____'s dirty.

That's why I like to clean.

Even _____, on my birthday,

A clean _____ is my dream!

bonjour, hello, hi, shrimp, book, fish, clean, dirty, worm, yesterday, today, lake, river

OCEAN CREATURES

A shrimp has many legs! It has ten legs for walking, ten legs for swimming, and six legs for eating.

How many legs does a shrimp have all together?

Draw your answer.

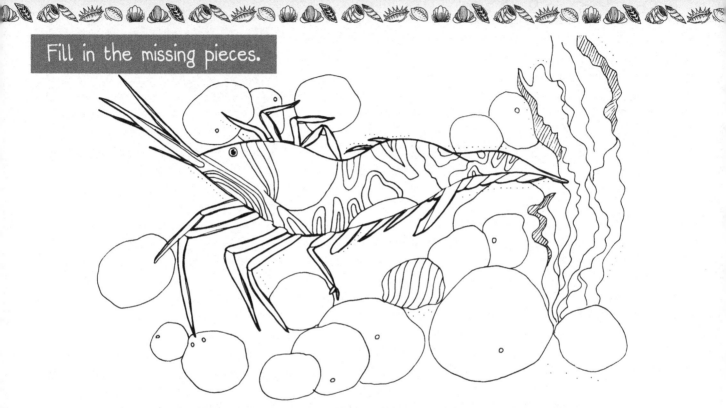

Fill in the missing pieces.

THE SHRIMP

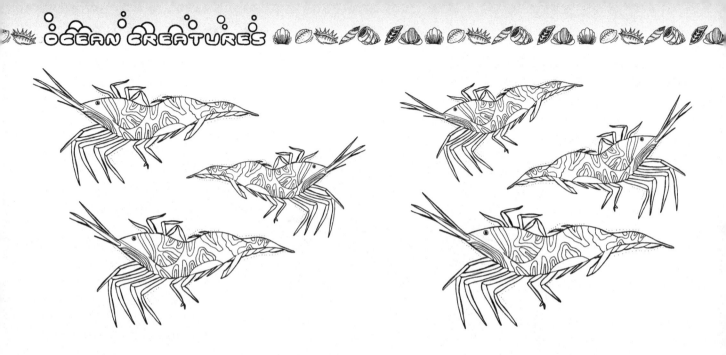

Anna, Trevon, Edmund, and Grace went fishing and are using shrimp as bait. They each have three shrimp. How many shrimp do they have together?

Write your answer here: _____

4 * 3

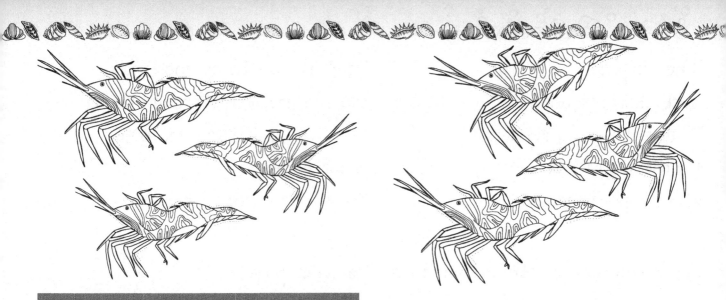

Dive deeper with these activities!

Do you like to eat shrimp? You'll never know unless you try it! Look for a recipe for fried shrimp on AllRecipes.com and try making it with an adult!

Sea Monkeys and Aqua Dragons are actually a type of brine shrimp. Ask an adult about getting a brine shrimp aquarium!

The Dolphin

"Click, click — squeal!"

That's definitely my sound!

It's the way I talk

When I splash around

Dolphins love to do cool tricks

We flip and jump through hoops

We smile and laugh and play

great games

And swim in loop — de — loops!

Fill in the spaces with the words on the next page.

"Click, click — squeal!"

That's_____ my sound!

 It's the way I talk

When I splash around

Dolphins love to do cool tricks

We flip and jump through _____

We smile and _____ and play

_____ _____

And swim in loop — de — loops!

definitely, not, rock, fern, coral, toys, cars, hoops, cry, laugh, games, boring, great

Dolphins love to jump through hoops and play with balls. At the dolphin pool, there are two hoops and four balls. How many hoops and balls are there together?

Draw your answer.

Find the differences.

THE DOLPHIN

Dolphins are very helpful animals. Even in the wild, they like to interact with humans and have saved people from sharks! Lead the dolphins through the maze, so that they can help the divers get home!

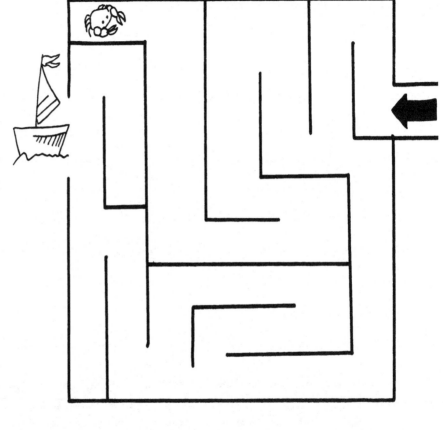

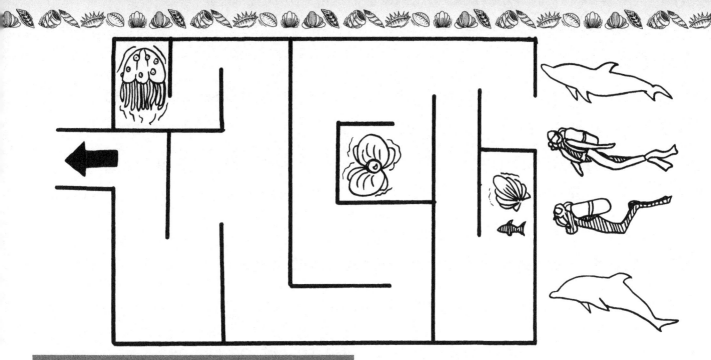

Dive deeper with these activities!

Dolphins can be taught to do amazing tricks! Ask an adult to help you look up "dolphin training" on YouTube.

Go to your local library and check out a book on dolphins!

OCEAN CREATURES

The Octopus

The "Octo" in my name means "eight"
Eight legs is what I call "just great"!
With two eyes and a funny face
I swim all over the place

I have suckers, so I can grab
Fish to eat or maybe crab
Things like that are in my lunch
"Mmmm, mmm!" Munch, munch, munch!

Fill in the spaces with the words on the next page.

The "Octo" in my name means "eight"
_____ legs is what I call "just _____"!
With two eyes and a funny _____
I swim all over the place

I have _____, so I can grab
Fish to eat or maybe _____
Things like that are in my _____
"Mmmm, mmm!" Munch, munch, munch!

ten, eight, fourteen, fine, great, face, nose, hands, suckers, hamburgers, crab, dinner, lunch

Octopuses have eight legs. If there are two octopuses, how many legs will there be?

Draw your answer.

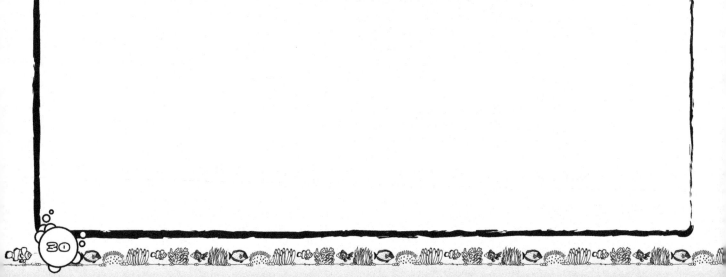

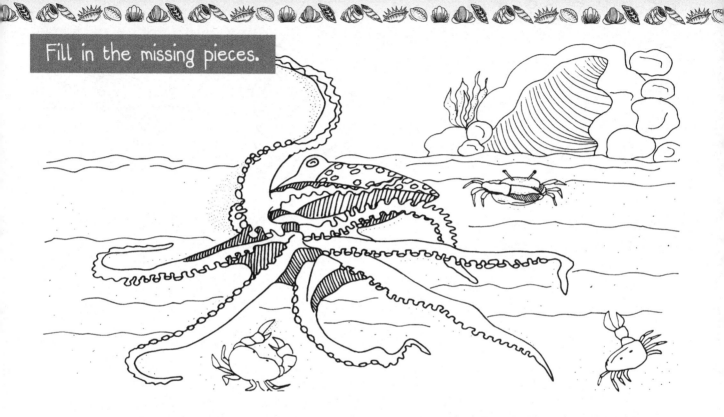

Fill in the missing pieces.

THE OCTOPUS

Octopuses love to eat crabs! Here are four groups of four crabs.

How many crabs are there?

Write your answer here: _____

4 × 4

Octopuses are some of the smartest animals! Watch a documentary about them and share your favorite facts from what you learned with a friend!

There is an octopus that can copy the look and behavior of other animals! Look up the "mimmic octopus" on WikiPedia. You'll be amazed by what you find!

The Sea Cucumber

Sea cucumber is my name
Although I'm not a plant
The vegetable that shares my fame,
I swim, but no — he can't!

I live down at the ocean floor,
Where it's cold and dark.
I don't like it up where it's warm,
'Cause there could be a shark!

Fill in the spaces with the words on the next page.

Sea _____ is my name

Although I'm not a _____

The _____ that shares my fame

I _____, but no — he can't!

I live down at the _____ floor,

Where it's cold and dark.

I don't like it up where it's warm,

'Cause there could be a _____!

34

lettuce, sea cucumber, tomato, plant, animal, vegetable, wallet, horn, walk, swim, ocean, lake, store, shark, car salesman

OCEAN CREATURES

Marine biologists in a submersible, a small submarine, travel all the way to the ocean floor. They see three different kinds of sea cucumber: five long, thin Hawaiian sea cucumbers, two Spanish dancer sea cucmbers, and two more king sea cucumbers. How many sea cucumbers did they see?

Draw your answer.

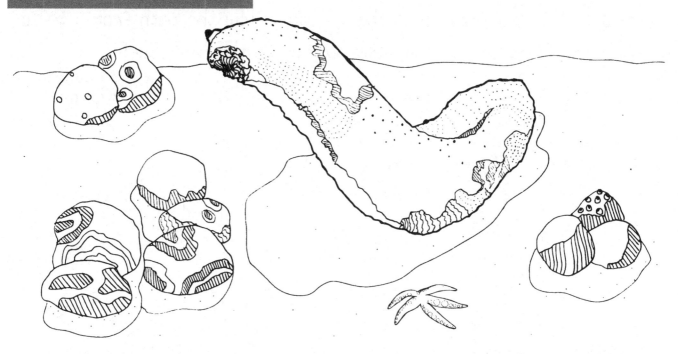

THE SEA CUCUMBER

Some sea cucumbers, like Pelagothuria natatrix, swim instead of just crawling on the sea floor! Help this one to follow the path from 1 to 20 on the page. Draw a line from each number to the next one!

Dive deeper with these activities!

In some places around the Pacific Ocean, like China, Indonesia, Japan, and Hawaii, the sea cucumber is considered a delicacy! Look up two sea cucumber recipes online!

Pearlfish and some sea cucumbers have a crazy relationship! Look them both up on WikiPedia to find out what it is!

The Jellyfish

Stay away from me, my friend,
Unless you want some pain!
I'm a jellyfish — ow!
My stingers make that plain.

Tentacles are my arms.
Sometimes I seem to fly.
My friends like to swim in swarms,
And if I touch you, you may cry!

Fill in the spaces with the words on the next page.

_____ away from me, my friend,

Unless you want some pain!

I am a _____ — ow!

My _____ make that plain.

_____ are my arms.

Sometimes I seem to _____.

My friends like to swim in _____,

And if I _____ you, you may ____!

40

swim, stay, jelly fish, owl, books, pictures, stingers, fingers, toes, tentacles, legs, elbows, fly, dance, sing, swarms, groups, pods, touch, punch, laugh, cry

Two sea divers, Emily and Susan, are swimming through the ocean when they see a swarm of jellyfish. Emily counts twelve pink jellyfish, and Susan counts eight blue jellyfish. How many jellyfish are there together?

Draw your answer.

Fill in the missing pieces.

THE JELLYFISH

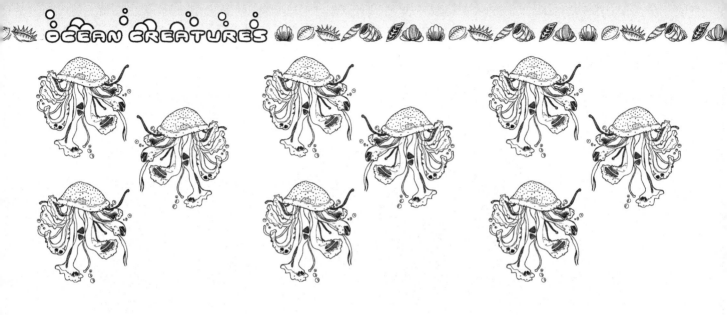

Oh, look: a swarm of jellyfish! There are six groups of three jellyfish. How many jellyfish are there?

Write your answer here: _____

6 * 3

Dive deeper with these activities!

Box jellyfish are one of the most poisonous animals in the world! Look them up on Wikipedia to find out more!

Jellyfish don't have a brain, and yet they can swim! Some of them can even see what is around them! Watch a documentary about them and share the interesting facts you find with an adult!

The Clownfish

Clownfish is my name.

I tell ya' — it's no joke!

I live in an anemone,

A very stingey bloke

My friends and I, who live here,

Are just used to it,

But other fish, when they get stung,

They yell and say, "Hey — quit!"

Fill in the spaces with the words on the next page.

_____ is my name.

I tell ya' — it's no _____!

I live in an _____,

A very stingey bloke

My _____ and I, who live here,

Are just used to it,

But other fish, when they get _____,

They yell and say, "Hey — quit!"

Spelling Words

Clownfish, Joke, Anemone, Singey, Sting, Stung

clownfish, Harrold, Kevin, turtle, joke, jellyfish, house, anemone, box, friends, buddies, enemies, stung, hurt, cereal

47

Keren and her friend Harold go snorkeling off of the coast of Australia. They see a neighborhood of anemones with clownfish living in them. There are four anemones with two clownfish in each. How many clownfish are there?

Draw your answer.

THE CLOWNFISH

Color the clownfish!

Another name for clownfish is "anemone fish", because of their relationship with anemones. Look up anemones on Wikipedia to find out more about this strange animal that acts like a plant.

Watch "Finding Nemo" and make a list of as many fish as you can identify. Look those fish up in Wikipedia. Draw a picture above of your favorite fish from that movie.

The Seahorse

Seahorses are a curious folk.
They come in different colors.
Guess who carries their little ones —
A hint — it's not the mothers!

The eggs hatch in a little pouch,
That's inside daddy's tummy!
Then they leave when they pop out,
Looking for something yummy!

Fill in the spaces with the words on the next page.

_____ are a curious folk.

They come in different _____.

Guess who carries their little ones —

A hint — it's not the _____!

The eggs hatch in a little _____,

That's inside daddy's tummy!

Then they leave when they pop out,

Looking for something _____!

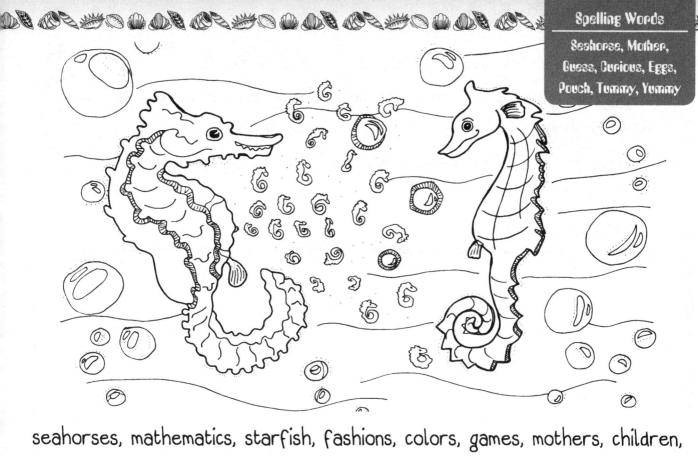

seahorses, mathematics, starfish, fashions, colors, games, mothers, children, daddies, pouch, punch, pillow, yummy, colorful, wild

Two seahorse families live together on a piece of coral.
The first family has a mommy seahorse, a daddy seahorse, and
five baby seahorses. The second has a mommy seahorse, a
daddy seahorse, and seven baby seahorses. How many seahorses
are there all together?

Draw your answer.

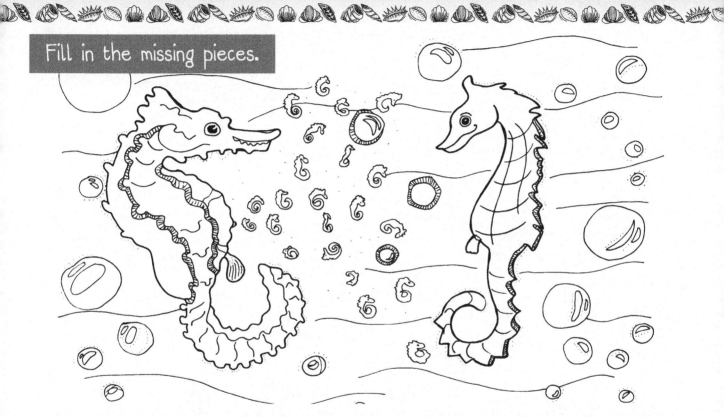

Fill in the missing pieces.

THE SEAHORSE

Oh no! Mommy and Daddy seahorse have lost their babies! Help them find 22 baby seahorses in this picture. You can color it when you are done.

The dwarf seahorse is one of the slowest moving fish in the ocean! It moves only five feet (152cm) per hour! To see what this feels like, get a timer and a tape measure. Measure out 5 feet and shuffle your feet to see if you can move that far in exactly one minute!

Go to your local library and get a book about seahorses to learn more!

The Starfish

Yup — you guessed it — I run this show!
I'm pretty much the star.
But ask me for a song and dance,
And you won't get very far!

Yes, I know — I have five legs,
Which is more than all of you.
But those are actually my arms!
My feet are out of view.

Fill in the spaces with the words on the next page.

Yup — you _____ it — I run this show!

I'm pretty much the _____.

But ask me for a song and dance,

And you won't get very _____!

Yes, I know — I have five _____,

Which is more than all of you.

But those are actually my _____!

My feet are out of _____.

guessed, told, walked, ran, star, boss, book, land, near, far, legs, arms, feet, toes, knees, view, angle, couch

Not all starfish have five arms! Some of them have seven, ten, or even fifty! Three starfish, Sally, Sam, and Sergio, all get together to have some soup. Sally has five arms, Sam has seven, and Sergio has ten.

How many arms do they have all together?

Draw your answer.

Fill in the missing pieces.

THE STARFISH

A bunch of starfish washed up on shore! There are five groups of five starfish. How many are there together?

Write your answer here: _____

5 × 5

Another animal that looks like a starfish is the brittle star. They have five arms, however, unlike starfish, they use them to move around. Look up "Brittle Star" on Wikipedia to find out more!

Some starfish have the ability to regrow arms if a predator eats one of them. Watch a documentary about starfish to find out more!

The Whale

I'm a whale, and that's my tail.
It's powerful and wide!
When more than one, we're called a "pod".
We swim against the tide.

There's nothing bigger on the earth,
Than a whale that's blue!
I'm sure you'd feel pretty small,
If I was next to you!

Fill in the spaces with the words on the next page.

I'm a whale, and that is my _____.

It's powerful and _____!

When more than one, we're

called a "_____".

We swim against the _____.

There's nothing _____ on the earth,

Than a whale that's _____ !

I'm sure you'd feel pretty small,

If I was _____ to you!

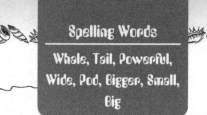

tail, tale, tea, porcupine, wide, narrow, long, pod, rod, fleet, tide, ocean, bigger, smaller, wider, blue, green, yellow, next, given, back

Three pods of whales meet. There are three sperm whales, two blue whales, and five humpback whales. How many whales are there together?

Draw your answer.

66

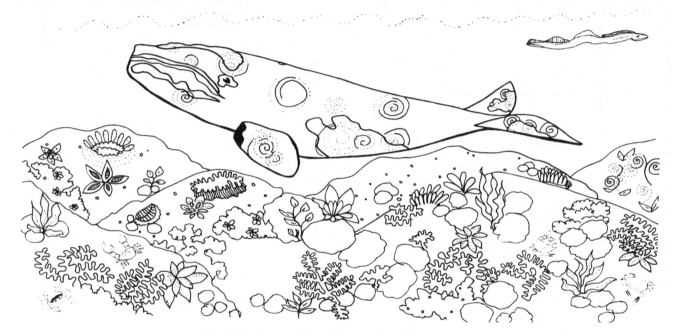

Find the differences.

THE WHALE

67

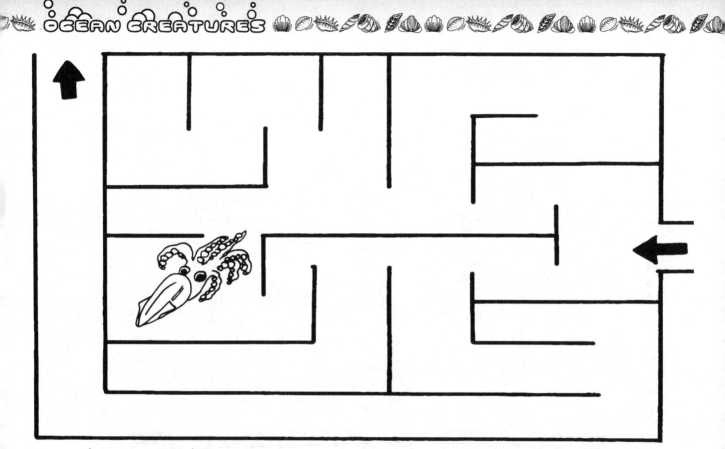

Help the sperm whale find a giant squid to eat and come back up for air!

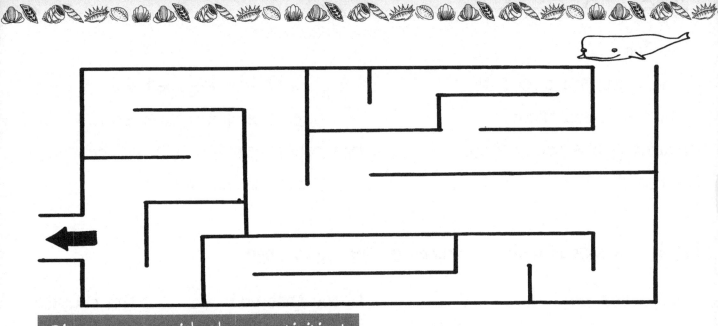

Dive deeper with these activities!

Ask an adult to help you search YouTube to hear how whales talk to each other!
Blue whales can be 98 feet (29.9 meters) long! Measure yourself and divide the
whale's length by that number. How many of you it would take to be as long as a
blue whale? Write your answer here: _____

69

The End

Tuna, bass, and swordfish,
Angel, carp, and trout.
Showing you a couple fish,
Is what this book's about!

I hope that you enjoyed this rhyme,
Through the great blue sea!
And hope again you'll have the time,
To come and visit me!

Fill in the spaces with the words on the next page.

Tuna, bass, and _____,

Angel, _____, and trout.

Showing you a _____ fish,

Is what this book's about!

I hope that you _____ this rhyme,

Through the great blue _____!

And hope again you'll have the _____,

To come and _____ me!

swordfish, car, ocean, chair, table, carp, hundred, couple, few, enjoyed, loved, read, sea, road, city, time, ability, house, visit, call, write

Two clownfish, a blue tang, three sharks, and five sea turtles get together to have a party. How many fish are there all together?

Draw your answer.

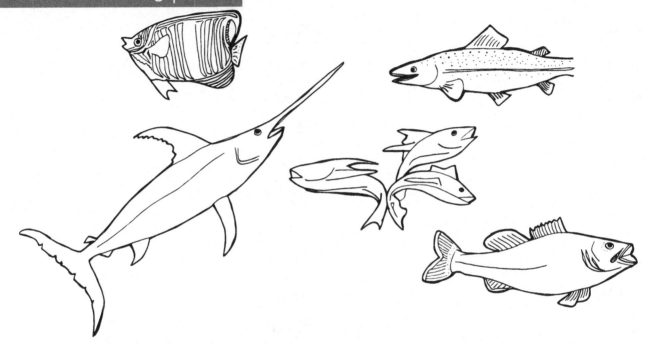

FISH ARE FUN!

Match the rhyming pairs:

Trout	Munch
Colors	Fame
Lunch	Shark
Pain	Plain
Sea	Cry
Name	Mothers
Star	Yummy
Dark	Far
Tummy	View
You	About
Fly	Me

Ask an adult to take you to the local city aquarium, where you can see real fish swimming around and ask the staff interesting questions!

Go back through the whole book and count the divers.
How many do you see?
Write your answer here: _____

OCEAN CREATURES

Math, Reading, Art, Science & Spelling Games
All About Ocean Creatures
Master 80 Interesting Spelling Words
Practice Simple Addition and Multiplication

Author: David Snead

Illustrations: Anna Kidalova

Designer: Feodor Zubrytsky

Published by: Sarah Brown

www.funschoolingbooks.com

Made in the USA
Columbia, SC
29 October 2020